Bipolar Disorder

A Guide to Understanding and Managing Bipolar Disorder

Table of Contents

Introduction

Any doctor or medical professional can look at a mental illness using the knowledge they have acquired over their many years of practice and give advice on how to manage it, but how do you recognize the symptoms and find treatment as a normal, everyday person? How do you recognize the signs of an oncoming collision of severe mood swings, weeks without sleep, and even worse, the lack of knowing when to reach out for help?

Those with undiagnosed or untreated bipolar disorder don't tend to think very clearly during a time of heightened emotions, which sadly often leaves a trail of destruction behind them. Their family members may be stressed out and confused as to why they are behaving this way when they were just fine the day before, and further scramble to fix the broken pieces their loved one left behind.

This is just one of many scenarios that someone dealing with the symptoms of bipolar disorder may be forced to face each day. The results of leaving the symptoms untreated can be scary, and sometimes dangerous, for both the person and their loved ones. However, there is still a shining light at the end of what appears to be a dark and impossible tunnel. Recovery and control over the symptoms of bipolar disorder is possible with proper treatment, a commitment to getting better, and the love and support of family and friends.

This book is not a guide to be used for doctors and nurses filled to the brim with expansive medical terminology and case studies; but is rather a resource for those just trying to love and support themselves or, help a loved one win the battle against bipolar disorder.

Chapter 1: What Is Bipolar Disorder?

The mental illness commonly referred to as bipolar disorder, is talked about throughout society and on television shows, but is very rarely depicted correctly. You see someone acting irrationally and going out of their way to hurt people, or as the suspect in a brutal crime. These depictions just increase the stigma for people that are already fighting a tough battle against their own brain. Maybe if everyone knew what this mental illness entailed and what the people suffering from it are actually going through, they would be more supportive and encouraging of those desperately seeking help.

So What Is Bipolar Disorder Exactly?

Bipolar disorder is an often severe, and lifelong mental condition that is in simple terms considered to be an emotional rollercoaster of ups and downs.

The ups and downs on this roller coaster are called mania and depression. The extreme mood swings and the toll that it takes can affect every part of someone's life. They affect their quality of sleep and their energy levels. They affect their attention and focus while causing the inability to think clearly, and consequently, affect their behavior and judgment. All of these aspects can cause issues with their work or school performance as well as within their personal relationships. Their confidence and self-esteem can easily be destroyed, often taking their social life with it. When people are unable to think clearly, they can make some bad judgment calls that can lead them into financial and legal problems.

Everyone has experienced depressive feelings at least once in their lives. Otherwise often recognized as the exhausting feelings of sadness and loneliness, such behavior greatly affects one's ability to be social and personal with those around them despite one's inner desire to do so. These feelings of being a burden can make you want to just lock yourself away from all of society.

Mania is on the opposite end of the mood spectrum of depression. It's like drinking 50 energy drinks at once and then free falling from a skyscraper. It's lying awake in bed all night with your eyes closed just waiting for the sun to come up, and still having the drive and energy to have a frantic day full of activities the next day. It's being so excited to tell someone a story that you forget to take a breath. It's working out for three hours straight and still having endless energy left over. It's the racing heart and the inability to sit still when you are trying to relax. It's the random intrusive thoughts carrying your conversations in every direction but the intended point of the story. Sometimes, those intrusive thoughts can be so extreme that they bring out hallucinations and delusions. Sometimes the thoughts turn so frightening that you need to be hospitalized for your own safety. After every free fall there is a crash, and as high as that skyscraper was is how low you are going to fall when you hit rock bottom. The destruction that was caused throughout the fall will have consequences, and sometimes the massive amounts of damage that was inflicted will leave you there to clean it up. Alone. Hopeless. Depressed.

Mania has a less intense little sister, named hypomania. The intensity and severity of becoming hypomanic is considered to be significantly less than a full manic episode. The likelihood of entering a state of psychosis is also lower than with mania. Hypomania can either be the beginning signs of a full manic episode or be a transition point when switching from a manic episode to a major depressive one.

The symptoms won't always be evident, and the mania and depression won't always be present. Depending on the person's stress levels and how well they manage their symptoms, someone with this mental illness can go long periods of time without a major mood episode. They may still have mood swings between these episodes, but they won't be as severe.

Is There a Difference Between Bipolar Disorder and Manic Depression?

The answer to this question is both yes and no. Manic depression was the original term for bipolar disorder going all the way back to Ancient Greece, when it was first used to describe the symptoms of all mental illnesses that were emotional or mood-based. Over time, the term 'manic' became stigmatized and less clinical. In the 1980s, the diagnosis was officially changed to bipolar disorder. You may hear the medical terms used interchangeably, but the correct vernacular is bipolar disorder.

Chapter 2: What are the Four Types of Bipolar Disorder?

If you are familiar with Bipolar Disorder, then you are most likely familiar with bipolar disorder types one and two. However, the general public's knowledge of bipolar disorder only goes as far as type one and two. Not many people know that there are actually four different types of bipolar diagnoses, all with their own types of mood swings and symptoms. Thus, all of them come with different requirements or specific criteria in order to get a proper diagnosis.

Bipolar Disorder one

Someone with the first type of bipolar disorder has experienced at least one manic episode, followed by either a hypomanic or depressive episode. The shift in moods are very noticeable, and can become extremely dangerous if the person starts to begin the process of psychosis. A person that has this type of bipolar disorder may never experience a *major* depressive episode, but does experience depression after their manic episodes.

Bipolar Disorder two

Just because this type of bipolar disorder is type two, doesn't mean that it is a less severe or milder form of the condition compared to type one. It still causes significant impairments in the person's day-to-day life, and is a completely separate diagnosis. Someone with bipolar disorder two has experienced at least one major depressive episode and one hypomanic episode that lasted longer than two weeks. When the person experiencing these major depressive episodes decides to seek medical help, they may be misdiagnosed as only having depression because of the lack of mania. This is very common, and sadly, the person doesn't get the help that they need because their treatment is only focused on depression, rather than both the depression and hypomania.

Cyclothymic Disorder

This disorder is commonly known as cyclothymia, and is considered to be in the bipolar family. The symptoms are less severe than bipolar one and two, and are characterized as having many depressive and hypomanic episodes. The mood swings and shifts are noticeable compared to the person's normal behavior. Going from feeling amazing for a few days to crashing and feeling terrible the next, cyclothymia can be very difficult to live with. This disorder can disrupt the functionality of the person's day and can later become a diagnosis of bipolar one or two. It can also manifest into a comorbid condition with an anxiety disorder.

Bipolar Disorder "Other Specified" and "Unspecified"

If someone receives the diagnosis of bipolar disorder other specified and unspecified, it means that their symptoms or pattern of behavior don't necessarily meet the criteria of bipolar one, bipolar two, or cyclothymia. They still experience abnormal mood swings or elevations, but their symptoms are normally attached to other issues. They may feel these abnormal mood shifts due to alcohol or drug abuse problems. Some people may have other medical conditions that cause their symptoms, such as multiple sclerosis or Cushing's disease. The symptoms may cause a disturbance in their daily life, but still don't meet the criteria for a specific bipolar disorder diagnosis.

Chapter 3: What are the Symptoms to Look out for?

The warning signs of bipolar disorder are so much more than extreme and irrational mood swings. There is often a build-up of symptoms before the first severe mood episode even occurs. All four types of bipolar have the same symptoms, it just depends how often each of the symptoms occur and if all of those symptoms form a pattern of behaviors that fit a certain criterion.

Manic and Hypomanic Episodes

Abnormally Upbeat and Jumpy

During a manic episode, a person is considered unusually upbeat. Sometimes it seems like they have drunk all the coffee in the house and are abnormally jumpy and wired. While some people describe their mania as giving them extraordinary energy, some people describe an extreme level of irritability. Mania isn't always being over excited and energetic; it can be filled with anger and a constant feeling of irritation.

Less Need for Sleep

As mania progresses, the need for sleep becomes less and less. People describe that their brain just wanders throughout the night, or they stay up all night and work on projects because they have too much energy to just simply lay in bed. The projects that they start rarely get finished because something else grabs their attention, or they quickly become bored and start a new one.

Unusually Talkative and Fleeting Thoughts

Someone that is experiencing a full manic episode will use their excess energy to talk more than normal. Not only do they talk excessively, but they often speak too quickly to be understood. Their racing and fleeting thoughts make it difficult to stay on topic of the conversation, and they are constantly interrupted by their own thoughts, causing them to go in a completely different direction than what they were previously discussing.

More Prominent Addictive Behaviors and Feelings of Grandeur

People that already have an addictive personality may find some addicting behaviors more alluring in the throws of a manic episode. They may drink more often, and drink in larger quantities than they normally would. They may partake in using drugs, causing their symptoms to become amplified and last longer. Some people have the urge to go on shopping sprees and spend the money that they don't have on items that they don't need. They will buy random and expensive gifts for everyone they know, and rack up some serious debt along the way. Instead of spending unavailable money on shopping, some people choose to gamble. They spend hours in the casino until they have no choice but to leave because they have lost it all. Their false feelings of euphoria and heightened belief of self-confidence leads them to believe that they don't need to stop.

Risky Behaviors and Poor Decision Making

The addictive behavior that is exhibited goes hand-in-hand with the symptom of taking uncalculated risks and poor decision making. Sometimes these uncalculated risks lead to someone with bipolar disorder becoming hypersexual. Being hypersexual with multiple partners is risky enough, but they will often fail to think about protecting themselves, and the lack of protection often comes with unwanted consequences. Some women find themselves pregnant once their manic episode is over without knowledge of who the father is, and others find themselves needing to be tested for sexually transmitted diseases and infections due to the lack of protection used during sexual activity.

Hallucinations and Delusions

With the inability to sleep and the constant intrusive thoughts, the longer that a manic episode goes on the more likely it is that a person could go into a state of psychosis. The hallucinations and delusions of grandeur can become so extreme that the person becomes a danger to themselves and everyone around them. This is when hospitalization needs to be considered and calmly executed. Nobody wants to be locked in a room under observation for days at a time, but when it comes down to either living dangerously or becoming stable again, I'm sure your loved ones would rather see you get the help you need. All of the aforementioned symptoms can occur in a manic or hypomanic episode; however, a full manic episode requires at least three or more of these symptoms.

Depressive and Major Depressive Episodes

The criteria for a major depressive episode differs from that of a full manic episode. A manic episode requires three or more symptoms, or it is considered a hypomanic episode. A major depressive episode requires five or more symptoms, or it is only considered to be a depressive episode.

The symptoms of a depressive or major depressive episode are just as one would imagine depression feels. A person will feel an overwhelming feeling of sadness and hopelessness. They may become abnormally emotional over the smallest inconveniences, and cry frequently. They also may become irritated more easily instead of being weepy or tearful. The irritability is found to happen more often in teenagers, who tend to be irritated by things more often as a result of their drastic shift in hormones.

Loss of Interest in Hobbies and Pleasure of Activities

Things that used to make you happy to participate in may not be of interest to you anymore. The television shows that you used to love watching with your family have become dull and meaningless. All of the projects that you started during your last burst of energy or manic episode look stupid, and you have no ability to sit down and finish them. You don't want to play sports or exercise, in fact, you don't want to do anything that requires you leaving your bed.

Significant Weight Gain or Loss

Weight could go in either direction during a depressive episode. While some people feel insatiable during a depressive episode, others lose their appetite completely. The constant binge eating can cause major weight gain, leading the person to feel even worse about themselves. On the other end of the spectrum, the lack of energy to get up and eat can exacerbate the loss of appetite, causing the person to lose a large amount of weight and feel sick because they are becoming malnourished.

Sleeping Too Much or Insomnia

Just like weight, sleep can go to one extreme of the spectrum or the other. The idea of a sleep schedule goes right out the window when the person just wants to lay in bed and sleep all day. On the other end, some people find that their dark and depressing thoughts make sleep impossible, resulting in chronic insomnia. There may even be a time where you could experience both of these symptoms. You may sleep too much during the day, so when nighttime rolls around you are unable to sleep normally.

Restless or Noticeably Moving Slower

Depression can make some people feel restless. They feel the need to get up and do something but don't have the energy to do it. Some people notice that life seems to be moving slower than normal during a depressive episode. This slowness of life makes the person feel even more restless and exhausted.

Excessive Feelings of Inappropriate Guilt

Depression can make you feel guilty about everything and anything that happens in the world, even if it is not your fault. You may find yourself apologizing for everything under the sun and feel as if anything goes wrong it is automatically all your fault. Feeling at fault and blaming yourself for anything that happens only makes you feel worse, and can push you even further into the deep hole of depression.

Indecisiveness

A depressive episode can even make simple decisions feel complex. Do you want chicken or beef for dinner? You don't know. Do you want to wear red or blue today? You have no idea. Then you feel guilty and hopeless because you couldn't just make up your mind. If it is this hard to make up your mind for a simple choice, how hard is it going to be to make life altering decisions? How can a teenager decide if they want to go to college or go to work right after high school when they can't even decide what they should wear that day?

Isolation and Feeling Like a Burden

Feeling worthless and like a failure can make you feel like you are a burden for everyone in your life. You feel the need to isolate yourself so that they don't have to endure your meaningless existence anymore. It is easier to be alone than feel like your family is wasting their time trying to make you feel better. It is easier to pull your comforter over your head than listen to your loved ones beg you to get the help that you are not worthy of in the first place. You are unworthy of their worry and their love, life is just easier and quieter in isolation. So, you just sit in the dark and dwell on your overwhelming emotions.

Suicidal Ideation

Once someone in a major depressive state has fallen to the rock bottom of their deep hole, they have pushed everyone away and have fully isolated themselves, suicidal ideation might occur. At this point, they have come to believe their feelings of hopelessness and worthlessness to be true and accurate. They may start to feel like death is their only escape from the internal pain that they feel on a daily basis. They may begin to think about it regularly, which is then often followed by making a plan, and finally can culminate in attempting to take their own life. At this point, hospitalization is usually the only way to ensure their safety and recovery.

Symptoms in Children and Teens

The symptoms of bipolar disorder are harder to decipher with children and teenagers. Parents and doctors find it difficult to decide whether their rapid mood swings are caused by a mental illness or if it's just their personality or changing hormones. Kids have an issue with being indecisive and making risky choices already. How do they know if it's a behavioral issue, immaturity, or a chemical imbalance? Doctors must be able to recognize a pattern of these behaviors in order to give them an accurate diagnosis, so it may take quite some time to get a bipolar diagnosis for a child or a teenager.

Chapter 4: How Is Bipolar Disorder Diagnosed?

Bipolar disorder is a mental condition that is with you for life, and the only way to be able to successfully move forward is to get the right treatment. The first step to getting this treatment is receiving a proper diagnosis.

Time for a Checkup

Once the red flags of bipolar disorder have been raised, how does one go about being diagnosed so they can start treatment? First, you'll need to make an appointment with your family doctor. I'm sure you are wondering why you wouldn't just call a therapist and make an appointment with them, but allow me to explain. Your family doctor will do a physical examination and conduct an interview where they will ask you about what symptoms you are experiencing. Your doctor will most likely order some blood tests. Bipolar disorder won't show up in your blood tests, but it will test for other illnesses or diseases that are going untreated that could affect your behavior, like thyroid disease.

After your blood test results come back and rule out any other illnesses, your doctor can refer you to a mental health professional. A mental health professional, such as a psychologist or a psychiatrist, will ask you about your symptoms and take note of your pattern of behaviors. They will also ask you about how these symptoms are affecting and having an impact on your life.

Diagnosis for Bipolar one

Bipolar disorder one is diagnosed when a manic episode has lasted longer than a week. It may also be diagnosed if the episode lasted less than a week but was severe enough to cause you to be hospitalized. You don't necessarily need a depressive episode with this diagnosis as bipolar one only requires a full manic episode to meet the criteria.

Diagnosis for Bipolar two

Bipolar disorder two is diagnosed when a major depressive episode switches back and forth with hypomania for longer than a period of two weeks. Remember that bipolar two doesn't require a full manic episode. If someone experiences a full manic episode they would meet the criteria for bipolar one with what is considered a "mixed" episode.

Diagnosis for Cyclothymic Disorder

Cyclothymic disorder, or cyclothymia, is diagnosed when someone has consistent, but unstable, cycles of depressive and hypomanic episodes. The cycles have to run for at least two years; however, it is diagnosed in children and teenagers after just one year. For a proper diagnosis, the periods of these unstable cycles have to last for less than eight weeks.

Diagnosis for Bipolar Disorder "Other Specified" or "Unspecified"

The diagnosis for bipolar disorder "other specified" is a little bit trickier. People that have this type don't fit the criteria for any other type of bipolar disorder, but experience mood swings that are considered abnormal for them. A medical professional will keep a watchful eye on them to make sure that their symptoms don't become bipolar type one or two.

Comorbid Medical Conditions

There are quite a few medical conditions that may come along with a bipolar disorder diagnosis. Some of the disorders take place within other parts of your body, while some are other mental illnesses that might come along with your symptoms.

An anxiety disorder is a common diagnosis that goes along with bipolar disorder. Anxiety can cause impairments in anyone's day, and make the day-to-day functioning of someone with bipolar disorder even more disrupted. Insomnia is a symptom of anxiety and the difficulty of finding adequate sleep can cause a significant amount of stress on the body, triggering a manic episode. The additional stress from the possibility of a panic or anxiety attack can make someone isolate themselves even more during a depressive episode. An anxiety disorder may not be diagnosed right away, but you may feel more sensitive to your level of anxiety once medication is added to your daily regimen.

Eating disorders aren't rare with bipolar disorder, as many people become anxious or obsessed with the amount of food that they eat during a depressive episode. Many people diagnosed with bipolar disorder are considered to be overweight and are more susceptible to diabetes and hypertension. Weight can become an issue when someone begins to binge eat during a state of depression, or as a side effect of their medication if it causes them to have an increased appetite. A depressive episode may do the opposite for someone else and cause them to stop eating completely, which makes them lose a significant amount of weight at an unhealthy pace. The obsession with weight often continues until other medical issues present themselves, such as dehydration and malnutrition, prompting further medical care.

Attention-deficit/hyperactivity disorder (ADHD) may seem like it's unrelated but has been found to be very prominent within the bipolar community. The inability to focus due to other symptoms and the overactive brain from a manic episode are the perfect recipe to result in ADHD.

Heart disease, thyroid problems, and chronic headaches or migraines are medical issues that are found to be comorbid with bipolar disorder. The risks of becoming obese due to overeating can impact your heart health and is only pushed further along by a dysfunction within the thyroid. Side effects of some medications cause cardiovascular issues that can lead to chronic headaches, migraines, and possibly a stroke. If treatment is causing you to gain weight, you may need to have your prescribing doctor change your medication before the side effects cause more issues down the line for you.

Chapter 5: What are the Causes and Risk Factors of Bipolar Disorder?

The symptoms of bipolar disorder may seem to come out of nowhere, but what are the causes of someone actually having this mental illness? Were they born with a predisposition and after a certain amount of stress the symptoms just appear? Is it something you did unintentionally that made this condition develop over time? Are there certain risk factors that can increase the possibility of your first major mood episode?

The Causes

The exact cause of what gives one person a mental illness, such as bipolar disorder, rather than someone else is still unknown. Doctors believe that it could be any number of combined factors that cause someone to develop bipolar disorder. Some of these factors could be biological components, genetic predisposition, or environmental causes.

Could it be Biological?

A biological component could be the reason behind why someone is more likely to be bipolar than another. A brain's faulty wiring and the lower levels of chemicals transmitted throughout the brain can make it unable to regulate their mood fluctuations. These chemicals are commonly known as neurotransmitters, and are made up of noradrenaline, dopamine, and serotonin. After studying the difference of a person's brain with bipolar disorder and one without the disorder, doctors came to the conclusion that the imbalance of these chemicals caused a dysfunction within the brain.

Doctors also noticed what happens to the brain if bipolar disorder goes untreated. The longer that a person with bipolar disorder goes without treatment, the more damage is done to their brain with each mood episode. Every manic and depressive episode that a person goes through without treatment can cause long term issues with their memory recall, ability to pay attention, their ability to make a successful connection to the outside world, their problem-solving skills, and the processing speed that allows them to absorb and understand new information. The results of these long term impairments cause more stress on the brain and the body, and cause mood episodes to last longer, become more severe, and occur more frequently.

Could It Be Genetics?

Being predisposed to having a severe mental condition like bipolar disorder seems to be very likely. The disorder is known to move along generations of family members. It is common to see multiple first-degree relatives in the same family have bipolar disorder. It is also not uncommon to see a set of twins with bipolar disorder. If one has been diagnosed with bipolar disorder, the likelihood that the other twin has it is increased significantly.

Could it be Environmental or a Combination of the Three?

Even if someone is genetically predisposed or has the biological components to develop bipolar disorder, that doesn't necessarily mean that they will have it. However, with the right combination of genetics, biological impairments, and environmental stressors it could cause a perfect storm for a major mood episode.

What Risk Factors Could be the First Step Towards a Mood Episode?

Of course, having a first-degree blood relative that has bipolar is one major risk factor. However, dealing with high stress levels that cause emotions that are difficult to regulate can give someone a push towards a major mood episode. Periods of high stress, sometimes caused by a traumatic event or the death of a close family member or friend, can indeed send someone over the edge. The use of drugs and alcohol also magnifies the possibility of having a manic or depressive episode to an even higher degree. Even though doctors don't know what exactly causes someone to have bipolar disorder, by knowing your family medical history and working to manage your stress levels, you can pay close attention to any red flags or symptoms that may arise.

Chapter 6: How is Bipolar Disorder Normally Treated?

After a proper diagnosis of bipolar disorder, a treatment plan will be put in place. There are so many moving parts in a treatment plan. There are some that require the help of medical professionals, and some that require you to do the work on your own. Being fully committed to your recovery doesn't mean it will automatically be a quick fix. Sometimes your medicine will need to be readjusted or switched out for something else due to side effects. Sometimes therapy can start to make you feel worse before you start to feel better, but sticking with the treatment is a lifelong commitment— even if it gets rough sometimes.

It is of utmost importance to start treatment as soon as possible, as your symptoms will only get worse the longer that they are left untreated. Waiting to get better on your own is dangerous and can have severe consequences in regard to your health, relationships, and work or school performance.

Psychotherapy

There are multiple types of psychotherapy that are utilized within a treatment plan for bipolar disorder. Each type of therapy focuses on different aspects of how to handle the symptoms and how they affect your daily life. Being able to express how you are feeling and what to do with those emotions can efficiently lower your stress level and ensure that you progress towards recovery.

Cognitive Behavioral Therapy

Cognitive behavioral therapy (CBT) is used to change your negative thinking patterns and behaviors into positive ones. It will teach you how to identify and use coping strategies in order to deal with negative thought and behavioral patterns. After identifying the patterns and using the coping strategies, you will then be able to break and replace the patterns with new, positive ones. In a study, people that participated in CBT sessions that lasted longer than 90 minutes each showed a vast improvement in their mood regulation and breaking of destructive behavioral patterns.

Family-Focused Therapy

Family-focused therapy isn't always all about your family, as the name suggests. Rather, this type of therapy is used as an educational resource that the person and their loved ones can use to be educated about mental illness and putting a treatment plan into place. Even though the therapist will focus on the patient that has bipolar disorder and the symptoms they are exhibiting, the therapist will also welcome input from family members or close friends that the patient may not notice or is afraid to say out loud. Educating yourself and your family members about the complexity of bipolar disorder and its symptoms creates a higher probability for successful treatment and recovery.

ElectroConvulsive Therapy

ElectroConvulsive Therapy (ECT), or electroshock therapy, is a type of treatment that is used very rarely. It has been used as a short-term treatment for people with bipolar disorder that are extremely suicidal or are experiencing a full manic episode. The use of ECT isn't just for someone that is having a full manic episode, but rather for someone that has not shown any response to a number of treatments. Patients that require ECT have not shown any progress with medication to treat the symptoms of their mania or major depressive episode, or the symptoms have become so dangerous to themselves and others that they cannot wait until the medication takes full effect.

Medications Used During Treatment

Along with the use of psychotherapy, your treatment plan may include one specific type of medication or a combination of a few different ones. These medications fall into three different categories: mood stabilizers, antipsychotics, and antidepressants. The medication or combination of medications that are added to your daily regimen are chosen for the effects they have on decreasing the severity of your symptoms. The side effects will also be taken into consideration, and your medication may have to be changed a few times before you and your doctor find what combination works best for you.

Mood Stabilizers

The purpose of a mood stabilizer during the treatment of bipolar disorder is to treat and prevent the manic and depressive episodes the person frequently suffers from. It does just as the name states - it is used to stabilize and regulate someone's moods. Medications, such as lithium, are used to treat bipolar and the mood episodes in order to prevent a relapse in symptoms. Lithium has also been shown to lower the risk of suicide in people with bipolar disorder.

Some medications are used by themselves or in combination with other medications to treat difficult mood episodes. The mood stabilizer, Carbamazepine, is often used to treat the extreme symptoms of mania that normally occur during the process of rapid cycling. Lamotrigine is used to treat all bipolar type one symptoms, but is used more specifically to treat the people that exhibit symptoms of bipolar depression.

Antipsychotics

The use of antipsychotics to treat both manic and depressive symptoms and episodes could be either long-term or short-term, depending on how severe and frequently the person exhibits these symptoms. They can be used short-term to treat and manage manic symptoms, or long-term for people that don't respond to other mood stabilizers. As the term 'antipsychotic' states, the purpose of this medication is to treat the psychotic symptoms one often experiences during a manic, depressive, or mixed episode. Some antipsychotics have been shown to stabilize moods, and act as a sedative for people with insomnia or high levels of agitation.

They also have the purpose of regulating one's brain function in regard to problem-solving, thinking clearly and perceptively, and attention to detail. Antipsychotics act quickly within the body to regulate positive thinking patterns and stop destructive behaviors attributed to manic episodes. The benefits of using antipsychotics don't come without unwanted side effects, however. Some of these medications cause weight gain and increase in appetite and cholesterol, while some can cause muscle tremors and drowsiness. Different medications vary in side effects in different people, so if the side effects become intolerable make sure to contact your doctor to see if a different medication can benefit you without the side effects.

Antidepressants

Antidepressants are an optional medication to be used to treat the depression one often experiences with their bipolar. Sometimes, the mood stabilizers that are prescribed to specifically help with bipolar depression aren't enough, and an antidepressant needs to be prescribed as well. However, antidepressants are prescribed with caution for someone that has bipolar disorder type one because they can cause a manic episode. Your doctor will be very cautious when prescribing antidepressants, and will give you strict instructions to call them immediately if any manic or psychotic symptoms begin to emerge after starting the medication.

The Importance of Medication

Medication is a very important part of your treatment plan, and using them as prescribed is the only way that they'll help you feel better. Many people try to stop taking the medication when they start to feel better, and tell themselves that they don't need help any longer or can manage on their own. Stopping your medication without medical supervision is extremely dangerous usually and causes your symptoms to come back and get worse. Quitting your medication all at once can cause withdrawal symptoms that will make you feel physically sick and mentally unstable.

Chapter 7: Alternative Treatments for Managing Symptoms

While you are treating your symptoms of bipolar disorder on the medical front, there are also some alternative treatments that can be used at home and in your everyday life to manage your symptoms. These treatments are not to be used to replace medical treatment, but to take your recovery farther in hopes to prevent a relapse. Bipolar disorder is a serious lifelong illness, as previously discussed, and is complex in nature to treat due to the need to treat two different types of symptoms. These alternative treatments can be used along with your professionally prescribed medical treatment to further reduce and prevent the symptoms attributed to mania and depression.

Vitamins to Promote Overall Wellness

Taking medication and participating in therapy are essential to a successful recovery and prevention of relapse, but so is being an advocate for your own health and doing your part to make your treatment work. Taking vitamins may not be a lifesaving treatment, but they are an alternative way to alleviate the symptoms that are exacerbated by mania and depression.

Omega-3 Fish Oils

Omega-3 fish oil has been commonly used to support heart health and the prevention of arthritis, especially in elderly people. It can be found in cod, salmon, tuna, and other types of fish, or it can be taken as a daily supplement in pill or gummy form. However, fish oil does so much more than support your heart and reduce arthritis inducing inflammation. For someone that has bipolar disorder, it can help stabilize your mood and help you focus and think clearly. Fish oil can also decrease the severity of your depression symptoms and cut down the length of a depressive episode.

B1 and B12 Vitamins

There are so many varying types of vitamin B that it is near impossible to keep straight which type holds what kind of benefits. For people with bipolar disorder, the best B vitamins to focus on are B1 and B12. Vitamin B1 helps ease the feelings of anxiety and irritability that often accompanies bipolar disorder, especially those that are diagnosed with the comorbidity of an anxiety disorder.

People that have a deficiency of B12 in their systems may have more issues than others with their energy levels, mood regulation, and more severe manic and depressive episodes. While a balanced diet can fix your deficiency, an added supplement can also bring a much needed energy boost to help you get through the day while keeping your moods more stabilized.

Magnesium

People with bipolar also often have a deficiency in a vitamin called magnesium. This deficiency can cause more anxiety, irritability, and insomnia during a manic episode. Magnesium is also used to treat anxiety induced tics by relaxing the body and it's nerves. This vitamin can be absorbed into your system with a well-balanced meal, and by taking a daily supplement.

Supplements and Vitamins to Avoid

Not all vitamins are the same, especially when you are treating certain bipolar symptoms. The last thing you want to do is make your symptoms worse when you are trying to alleviate them. The supplement, ginkgo biloba, has been shown to greatly improve one's short-term memory and focus, however, it can also make certain bipolar medications ineffective. Making your medicine ineffective is only going to hurt your progress and could result in a relapse of your symptoms.

The supplement, St. John's Wort can work wonders for people that are taking antidepressants to combat the symptoms of depression but should be used with extreme caution for someone with bipolar disorder. Just like a prescribing physician has to practice extreme caution when adding an antidepressant to a bipolar medication regimen, the result of using this supplement could be a full manic episode.

Meditation

Meditation has been practiced for centuries to gain the benefit of mindfulness and full body relaxation. Using deep breathing and positive affirmations to reduce one's anxieties and change their negative thought patterns has been found useful for millions of people around the world. All of these benefits are great, but how can relaxing your body and saying nice things about yourself help someone with bipolar disorder? Researchers have done plenty of studies, and even though the studies weren't focused on all of the symptoms of bipolar disorder, meditation and mindfulness have been shown to cause a vast improvement in many people's anxiety and depression symptoms. Being able to sit still and think positively about yourself during a depressive episode seems like it may be no easy feat, but teaching your body how to relax and live in the present can resolve your feelings of hopelessness. Focusing your attention on your breathing and the physical sensations of relaxation in your body can loosen the reins of the everyday guilt you are constantly plagued with. Gaining the ability to relax your overstimulated and tense body can conjure up the feeling of internal peace inside your brain, rather than eternal chaos that you have become accustomed to.

Meditation is not a one time quick fix for someone with bipolar disorder, nor is it a quick fix for anyone that doesn't have the condition. Introducing the practice of mindfulness into your daily schedule will teach you how to relax your natural impulses of constantly being on the run. Teaching your body that it is able to feel mentally and physically relaxed and less anxious can improve your quality of sleep, while lowering the frequency and severity of insomnia. The benefits happen over time, just like with your medical treatment. Being patient and making a commitment to get better are key.

Why Is Meditation Great for Alleviating Symptoms?

The reason that meditation is such a great alternative treatment to help alleviate your symptoms is the four major components of meditation: environment, posture, attention, and attitude. The environment that is needed for a successful meditation has to be a quiet location where the person can be undisturbed. People with bipolar disorder have a difficult time focusing on the task ahead if there are distractions around, so removing all distractions takes away the stress of their focus being pulled in another direction.

The postures required for meditation are not one of restriction, but one of comfort. Bipolar disorder can make it difficult to be comfortable and always feel the need to move around in order to feel that sensation. Focusing on what makes you comfortable and what helps you relax your body can help soothe the restless sensation of needing to get up and move around.

During your meditation, your attention is focused on your breath. You may find your mind wandering about to begin with, but over time you will learn to stop the intrusion and bring your focus back to your breathing. Being able to halt your racing thoughts and place your attention on where your focus should be tells your brain that you are in control, and over time you and your mind will start to believe it. You will remember that you hold the power over your thoughts when negative thinking patterns rears its ugly head in your direction. You will learn how to manage your negative thoughts and emotions and use that energy to be productive and positive. Focusing on your emotions and your positive affirmations during a peaceful meditation brings your attention to the present, rather than the anxieties of the future or the consequences of the past.

The last component of mindful meditation is attitude. Dealing with a brain riddled with negative thoughts about your life and yourself can be a real drain on your emotions and attitude. It is hard enough to listen to someone else berate you on a daily basis, but when it's your own thoughts doing it, how could you expect yourself to have an upbeat attitude? Saying positive things to yourself and creating a feeling of being open and accepting of your condition can bring forth a better attitude. Giving your emotions and negative feelings a place to be accepted without judging yourself creates an open space where you no longer need to feel ashamed of being you and having flaws.

Meditation for Beginners

The first step in learning to meditate is finding a quiet location. There are places that practice group meditation, such as yoga centers or athletic clubs, or you could practice in your own home. If you prefer to join a group meditation, your treatment team could give you a list of centers that have scheduled sessions. There are also plenty of apps on your phone that provide guided meditations to enjoy in the comfort of your own bedroom or living room, wherever you choose to be your quiet place. Some people find enjoyment by building their own comfortable place in the corner of their home. They fill their little space with comfortable blankets, pillows, sound machines, and essential oils that relax them. Whatever makes you feel more relaxed and able to proceed without being interrupted for about 10 to 15 minutes is perfect for a successful meditation. Put your phone on silent, turn off your television, and just allow yourself to be present without any distractions. You don't need to make a big deal or theatrical performance out of your location. Just find a recliner or a bed that allows you to relax. If you find yourself getting too tired while you are meditating in bed, choose a different location that allows you to sit up next time. Lay your hands comfortably in your lap and take a deep breath before you begin.

While on the subject of comfort, be sure to wear clothes that are light and nonrestrictive. You don't have to go out and buy special clothes - sweatpants and an oversized t-shirt will do. If you are meditating during your lunch hour at work, you could kick off your shoes and loosen your belt or tie. It is difficult to focus on becoming relaxed and deep breathing when you feel restricted and uncomfortable.

The second step is to decide what you plan to work on that day. Are your negative thoughts making you feel more depressed? Are you having more issues focusing on the task in front of you than normal? Knowing what your intentions are before your meditation can steer you in the right direction of what mantras and positive affirmations to use.

Next, you will close your eyes and follow the steps of your guided meditation. It may start with focusing on your breath or on relaxing your muscles. Beginners can expect their thoughts to wander. Just remember to hit the pause button on those fleeting thoughts and bring your focus back to your breath. Don't worry about doing it wrong or that you are incapable of sitting still for a long time. If you practice every day, you will make quick progress!

A simple technique to get you started on your relaxation is the body scan. Close your eyes and slowly scan your entire body, starting at your forehead and ending at the tips of your toes. Focus on the parts of your body that feel more tense than others and visualize them becoming relaxed. The purpose of the body scan is to bring your thoughts to the present and to notice how stress is affecting your body.

Start to focus on your breathing even more. Pay attention to how your body feels when it breathes and your lungs fill up with air, and then the sensation of pushing that air out. Focus your attention on the physical sensation of how your lungs feel during that pause between breaths. Your body knows how to breathe automatically without you having to give it a constant reminder, so don't try to control how you are breathing and just allow yourself to pay attention to the natural rhythm.

Once you are relaxed, start to state your positive affirmations or mantras specific to your intentions. The reason you use mantras and affirmations during meditation is to connect you with your main intention and what you want to change, so you can carry that positive thought and intent throughout your day. Mantras, such as "I control my emotions, they don't control me" or "I am stronger than my depression", connect you to how you feel and what you want to be true. The more you say them throughout the day during moments of uncomfortable emotions, the more you will start to believe them.

After your 10 to 15 minutes of meditation is over, get up and start your day with a new sense of purpose and connection to the world around you. When you find yourself beginning to feel stressed out throughout the day, restate your mantras and take a few deep breaths. The rest of the world can wait while you collect your thoughts.

Different Types of Therapy

Light Therapy

Someone with bipolar disorder may have a very difficult time maintaining a consistent sleep schedule. They may sleep too much during a depressive episode and not sleep at all during a manic episode. The inconsistency of how much and the quality of sleep they do receive can have an impact on their biological clock. The internal clock that would normally tell someone that it is time to go to sleep and when it has time to wake up has gone haywire, and can't tell the difference between the body's signals. Light therapy was designed to master reset this internal clock by using timed exposure to lightness and darkness for a prolonged amount of time. This master reset of the person's biological clock forces a change in their sleep schedule so that they can get quality sleep every night; consequently, lowering the amount of stress on their body and improving the management of their bipolar symptoms.

Interpersonal and Social Rhythm Therapy

Interpersonal and social rhythm therapy's main purpose is to teach you how to maintain a regular schedule. This includes creating a consistent schedule of when you eat, sleep, exercise, go to work, meditate, and so on. Making and maintaining a predictable schedule reduces stress and improves the daily functioning of the habits that bipolar disorder tends to disrupt.

A sleeping schedule consists of your nightly routine of what you do before you go to sleep. Maybe you eat a small snack at eight p.m., take a shower 15 minutes later, and be in bed by nine so you can wake up at seven a.m. to get ready for work. Your body may fight you at first, but following your schedule day after day will build a sense of stability.

Making an eating schedule and a meal plan takes all the guesswork out of what to eat, and when. Knowing what time you have to eat a meal and having the meal prepared and ready to go makes your day go a little smoother. Having a meal prepared for days in advance makes it easier to eat well balanced meals full of nutrients and vitamins, rather than going through the drive thru or bingeing on whatever you can find in the kitchen.

Adding exercise to your daily schedule has many benefits. Being active lowers the chances of becoming overweight and developing type two diabetes, which can be the result of an increased appetite due to your medication. Exercising promotes a balanced mood by burning the excess energy and irritability from a manic episode, or giving your serotonin levels a boost when you are feeling depressed.

A stable and well-balanced routine may make your life seem mundane and predictable, but predictability helps manage and lower your stress levels. The lower your stress levels, the more you are able to manage your symptoms to prevent a mood episode. Intentionally working on what you can control to prevent a manic or depressive episode may not stop all of the symptoms, but it will make them less severe and life easier to deal with.

Eye Movement Desensitization and Reprocessing Therapy

Bipolar patients with a history of trauma may find eye movement desensitization and reprocessing therapy, or EMDR, to be very beneficial in their recovery. EMDR is a therapeutic supervised program that is skillfully practiced by trained and licensed therapists. The therapy is specific to how the use of eye movements stimulate the brain when confronted with triggers and negative emotions attached to traumatic memories. This therapy is done in order to desensitize the person and reprocess the trigger or memory in a new and positive way. It differs from traditional talk therapy, where you are required to discuss your negative feelings and emotions, by taking those feelings and replacing them with positive ones.

EMDR requires the patient to focus their eyes on a moving external stimulus, like the therapist's finger, as they go over the memory and the negative feelings surrounding it. The focus on the stimuli while remembering a specific event causes both sides of the brain to be stimulated. Once the brain is stimulated, the therapist can take the identified negative feeling and trigger and replace it with a new one, changing how you feel when you remember that event.

Chapter 8: Helping Loved Ones With Bipolar

Maybe you are not the one that is fighting a never-ending battle with this mental illness. Perhaps it is your parent, spouse, sibling, or child. Seeing someone that you love struggle to grasp the reality of the situation, and refuse to get help can be heartbreaking. Trying to be the shoulder to cry on while holding the weight of the world on your back can be mind-numbing and confusing. Family members are usually the ones that have to deal with the consequences of their loved one's destructive actions during a manic episode. They are also the ones that have to pick up the slack when their spouse, child, parent, brother, or sister is too exhausted to complete their tasks during a depressive episode. However, no matter what they do or how they act, your love for them is unconditional. Taking a little bit of time out of your day to remind your loved one that you support them and their efforts to get better, can make a tough day a little more bearable.

Educate Yourself About the Condition

Taking the time to learn as much information as you can about bipolar disorder can change your perspective on why your loved one is acting this way. This valuable information and research can make you better equipped to deal with the extreme ups and downs. Helping them find certified doctors and therapists can ensure that they are getting the best help available. If they are having a difficult time and are resisting the need to call and make an appointment, you could set up the appointment and go with them. Simply showing up is a way to show them that you are supporting them through this process and that you love them, even if they aren't acting very loveable at the moment.

Going with them to their appointments can give you the opportunity to give their doctor or therapist better insight on their progress. People with bipolar disorder tend to be forgetful or don't notice how bad their symptoms have gotten, so a doctor may depend on their loved ones to fill in the blanks. Your loved one could be afraid that their behaviors and thoughts could have consequences, and don't feel safe telling their therapist that information. Having you there for emotional support can give them the strength needed to tell their doctor everything and get the proper help required.

Monitor Their Moods and Track Their Progress

Monitoring your loved ones' moods and any changes that you notice can provide many benefits. You can tell when they are building up to a manic episode and prepare yourself and your family. With time, you'll be able to tell if they are showing the signs of a full manic or depressive episode, or if they are just moody from a rough day. If one rough day turns into a rough week, you can be more watchful for other signs. The goal is to get ahead of the mood episode and figure out what is causing the added stress in their life. The further ahead of the issue you get, the more likely it is that you can take steps to help your loved one prevent mania or depression, or at least decrease the length and severity.

Keeping track of how far they have progressed also includes keeping track of their relapses. If you know how far your loved one has come since first starting treatment, you will know when they are beginning to backtrack. Relapsing is normal and is bound to happen, and once it starts to present itself it may be time for you to alert their doctor. If they are obviously backsliding in your presence, your loved one has probably been secretly backsliding for some time and was too afraid to say anything. They may not notice that their symptoms have even gotten out of hand because these mood swings, big and small, are normal for your loved one.

Learn About Their Medications and Possible Side Effects

Learning about your loved one's medications and what each one is for is very important. Sometimes they don't know what each one is for or what it treats, they just know that the doctor said to take it to feel better. Knowing what medications they take and what drug interactions to avoid could be lifesaving. If your loved one is in a crisis and an ambulance is called, you can notify EMT's what medication they are taking.

Educating yourself on what the possible side effects are with each medication can save your loved one and your family a lot of grief and trouble down the line. Some medications can cause a severe manic episode or make hallucinations worse. Some medications could make them feel extremely fatigued and unable to keep their eyes open, or increase their appetite so much that they can't stop eating. Other medications have the tendency to cause your loved one to have suicidal ideations and scary intrusive thoughts. Knowing what to look out for in the first few months of a medication regimen means staying ahead of any negative side effects. Normally doctors only start or adjust one medication at a time so if intolerable side effects do occur, they are able to decipher what caused it.

Encourage Them to Take Their Medication

Emphasizing the importance of taking medication can help them remember that they need it to keep up with their daily functions and progress. People that are being treated with medication for their bipolar disorder will start to feel better and think that the medication did its job, therefore, they no longer need to take their medicine. If they feel that the medication isn't working, your loved one may see no point in continuing their treatment. They may not be able to tolerate the side effects of taking their medication, as they may be gaining weight too quickly or are too tired to make it through the day. They would rather stop the medication than contact their doctor and have them change the dosage or move to a new medicine regimen. Reminding your loved one that their medication is important and calling their doctor if the medication needs to be recalibrated shows them that you care about their recovery and future success.

Recognize Early Symptoms

What do you do though before your parent, spouse, or child is diagnosed? What if they start acting strangely, in a way that they have never acted before? Perhaps your mother starts sleeping for long stretches of time or stops sleeping completely, and you often finding her deep cleaning the entire house at 3 a.m. Or, you notice that your husband is talking much more than they used to, and are speaking so fast that it seems they have to get the whole sentence out before they forget what they were going to say. Their mood has gotten dark and they would rather sit in their room with the lights off than spend quality time with the family. Maybe your child would rather be a recluse than spending time with their friends at the mall or park. Or, your brother or sister becomes more tearful than usual, and cries if you ask them a simple question or look at them a certain way.

Recognizing early signs of a mood episode when your loved one is already diagnosed makes the steps of preventing destructive behaviors more likely, but becoming aware of the early symptoms even before diagnosis can help you get your loved one the help they need. Finding treatment as soon as possible can save them and your family a lot of heartache and save everyone's sanity. Nobody wants to see their family member struggle to live a fulfilling life, and recognizing the signs and doing your research on why they are acting this way could be the first step in getting them the medical treatment they desperately need.

Communicate With Them

Healthy communication is a vital quality in any type of relationship. However, someone in the middle of full mania or major depression can be difficult to hold a conversation with. They lack the ability to comprehend what you are saying to them or understand why you care so much about how they are feeling. Even when you have the best intentions, you can get a great amount of resistance from your family member and possibly a door closed in your face.

The best time to talk to them is when you notice their body language is showing that they are open and calm. If they are hysterically crying or refuse to respond to you with their arms crossed over their body, it may not be the best time to talk. Wait until they seem relaxed, and then proceed to speak with them calmly. Tell your loved ones the signs you notice and ask them if they are okay or if they would like to talk about it. If they are open and willing to talk about their symptoms, you could discuss the steps that they need to take to get help so they don't feel this way anymore. The sooner they get help the better their progress will be. If you wait for them to get better on their own, the symptoms are only going to get worse, last longer, and become more destructive.

Don't be surprised if they are reluctant or refuse to seek medical treatment. Your loved one may tell you that nothing is wrong with them and they feel amazing, which is a common feeling during a manic episode. They may say that treatment is too much work and that they are too exhausted to even think about getting help right now if they are in a depressive mood episode. Your family member could even feel fearful of seeking help. What if they say the wrong thing or are so crazy that they get locked up in a mental institution, far away from their family and friends? Will the therapist just think that they are faking their symptoms because they like the attention? What if they are just acting like this because they want people to feel bad for them? Reminding them that their fears and feelings are valid will make them feel heard.

Let them know that even though you can't physically see their illness or condition doesn't make it any less severe than a condition they can see in the mirror. Just because your family member may not understand this concept right now, doesn't mean that one day in the near future it won't click and they will finally understand why it is important to take care of their mental health.

Offer Emotional Support

Starting a healthy conversation with your family member about their symptoms and seeking treatment is the first step in building a great emotional support system around them. Bipolar disorder has the tendency to make people feel like they have become a burden to the ones they love the most. Doing everything in your power to show them that this is the farthest from the truth reminds them that they are not alone and that they are very loved.

Make Time for Quality Time

Finding time to spend with your loved one can be difficult in the beginning. People with bipolar disorder often feel the need to isolate themselves when they are feeling depressed, and feel guilty for subjecting other people to their immense sadness. Sometimes you don't even need to speak to them. Just sitting with them on the couch while they watch their favorite movie shows them that you care and will make them more comfortable with your presence. The more comfortable with you that your family member becomes, the more willing they will be to talk to you when they are ready.

Find other ways to increase their level of comfortability with you. Go on daily walks with them when they are having a manic episode so they can burn off some extra energy. You could start doing yoga together, so that you can both benefit from the relaxation and mindfulness it provides. Try to slowly incorporate their former favorite activities into their lives and participate in them yourself. Don't be surprised if they are reluctant at first to spend quality time with you, but don't give up. Just keep trying and always remind them that you are always available when they are ready to spend time with you.

Find Ways to Reduce Their Stress Levels

Help your loved ones find new and innovative ways to reduce their stress. A high stress level is a key component to the beginning of a mood episode. Becoming anxious about an upcoming appointment or upset about a traumatic event can increase their stress and their symptoms can become more obvious to the people that see them on a daily basis. Finding more effective ways to reduce their daily stress can give them a better chance to deal with their symptoms when bigger events happen.

Working with your family member to make a daily schedule that is manageable and attainable makes their day more predictable. They may find it even better if the entire family had a daily schedule. The predictability of a routine schedule removes the stress of not knowing what is going on that day or for the rest of the week. Having an accessible monthly schedule that shows everyone in the household's appointments and upcoming events allows them to see what is going on and be prepared with what is coming up in the future.

If you have a time during the week when you are always available, you could volunteer to help them to complete some tasks or errands they need to run. They may be reluctant at first because they don't want to waste your time or seem like a burden, but in time they will be more accepting when they see you are trying to help them. Offering to help them clean their room or run around town to run errands can give them the company they secretly want while they fulfill their responsibilities.

Help your loved one find a new relaxing and productive hobby that you could do with them. Finding fulfillment in a new interest can help boost their mood and find comfort when they participate. Hobbies, like nature walks or painting, can be stimulating and creative outlets for their uncomfortable emotions. They could have a hidden talent that they never knew about, and finding something that they are good at can give them a self-esteem and confidence boost.

Remain Calm and Content During Emotional Outbursts

Watching someone that you love go through an emotional outburst can break your heart. You feel like you have to scream over their raised voice so that they can hear and understand what you are trying to say, as if a louder noise will suddenly calm them down. It may seem like a good idea at that time to debate or argue with everything they are saying, but your overwhelming emotions are clouding your judgment and stirring them up even more. Arguing with someone during an emotional outburst is counterproductive and does more harm than good.

People with bipolar disorder can become angry when they are confronted with their behavior or are asked to seek proper treatment. They will scream, throw things, and make threats to harm themselves or others. They want to get a reaction from you for making them so mad. Remaining calm during your loved one's emotional outbursts can seem impossible when they are screaming obscenities at you or demeaning you in every way possible. Remember that the goal to accomplish here is to get them to calm down and think rationally so that you can have a meaningful conversation with them. Becoming angry or discontent and joining their outburst will only push them further away from that goal.

When they are starting to raise their voice and vent their frustrations, just sit there and listen. Acknowledge what they are saying by nodding your head and allow them to keep going until they are all talked out. Don't respond unless they ask you for your opinion or it can seem like you are challenging their feelings or emotions. Staying calm and listening to them rant will make them feel heard and understood. Once they realize that you aren't going to add to the madness and are actually listening to their grievances, they will start to calm down and see that there is no reason for them to keep going with their outburst. You will feel tempted to show your emotions, but fight that temptation and remind yourself that this is for their own good. Letting them let go of their pent up emotions will allow them to peacefully collect themselves and eventually listen to you. When they are finally calm, both of you can start to work towards positive outcomes. However, if they become too hostile and don't show any signs of calming down, don't be afraid or feel guilty for calling emergency services.

Prepare Yourself for Destructive Behaviors

The first step towards any type of success is preparation. Preparing for destruction may not seem like success, but being prepared for the repercussions of your loved one's destructive behaviors means that you will know what to do if things go sour. It is your choice whether you include your loved one in this plan, but keeping them in the dark could make them feel distrustful towards you and other family members. Make a detailed plan with all involved family members about what to do if you notice that your loved one starts to display destructive behaviors.

When the detailed plan is made, make an agreement with the person while they are thinking clearly and rationally regarding what will happen if their symptoms start to flare up. Tell them clearly and concisely what things you will do, such as that you will take their keys and their credit cards, or that you will call their doctor on their behalf and let them know what is going on. If applicable for this person, perhaps you will take over the family financials. The reason that you want your family member to think rationally when you make this agreement is because you don't want them to think they are being punished for a mental illness that they have no control over. You are doing this for their benefit, so they don't hurt themselves or anyone else in the process.

Create a Crisis Management Plan

Nobody wants to believe they will need a plan for disaster, but being prepared for a crisis means you can get your loved one help promptly and effectively. While you plan your preparation for your loved one's destructive behaviors, also create a plan for what to do if they are in the middle of a crisis. Knowing exactly what to do in the moment can help you to react rationally rather than emotionally. Make a list of all of your family member's doctors and therapists with their phone numbers so that they can be called in case of an emergency. Put the list somewhere that it can be seen at all times—like the refrigerator. The last thing you want to do when time is of the essence is search the entire house for the list of phone numbers. Having the list visible at all times also allows the person to make the call themselves if they are home alone.

We can't be with our loved ones every second of the day, and eventually they will have to leave the house on their own. Making a list of their doctors, nurses, medications, and possible allergies to keep in their wallet or purse will become a valuable asset if they have a severe episode while they are in public. If they have to be admitted to the hospital or an ambulance is called, the doctor or EMT will know exactly who to get a hold of for medical information and diagnosis. The list of prescribed medications and allergies tells a doctor what they are dealing with and lowers the possibility of an adverse drug interaction.

Last, but most importantly, know when you need to call for help. If your loved one is suicidal or becomes a danger to you and your family, do not try to deal with it on your own. Call emergency services immediately and have them take care of it. Above all else, you want your loved one to be safe. Do not feel guilty about calling if you feel you need to.

Be Patient with Their Recovery Process

Even if your loved one is fully committed to getting better, relapses are still going to happen. Treatment is a trial and error process, meaning that medication that worked at first can lose its effectiveness over time. Being prescribed a certain medication to alleviate the symptoms doesn't always mean that that specific medication is going to work for them. Just because a specific research paper or scientific study shows that 95% of their patients showed an improvement in their symptoms, doesn't mean that your family member can't fall into that 5% that don't show improvement.

Recovery is something that has to be taken day by day. Some days will be amazing and your loved one will act just like they did before they exhibited symptoms; but some days can seem like it is the end of the world as their symptoms escalate. Remember, this isn't the end of the world though. It just means that their treatment plan needs to be readjusted or the medication needs to be changed out for something new. Treatment is not a quick fix for a lifelong condition, so be patient and go with the flow.

Be Supportive

Supporting your family member through all of their good and bad days and their treatment can be beneficial to their recovery. Someone that has bipolar disorder and lives in a household full of supportive family members will experience less stress and less mood episodes. Full support won't stop a manic or depressive episode, but they will experience milder symptoms. Feeling the full support of their family will make them more comfortable when they are talking about their symptoms and how they are feeling.

Be Accepting

Acceptance of your loved one's diagnosis is required in order to be supportive of their recovery. Knowing and fully acknowledging that you and your entire family's life isn't going to be the same as it used to be, and accepting that fact, is the first step in being supportive. Being accepting of the fact that they will have good days and bad days, and that treatment isn't always a direct path to recovery will change your perspective of what your new normal will be.

Accept Your Loved One's Limits

On their bad days, accept the fact that they cannot just pull themselves out of their mania or depression by choice. Accept that they can't always control their emotions or when they will have an episode. Instead, you can encourage them to use other alternative ways to cope and manage their symptoms. Exercise with them to boost that serotonin levels. Keep them on a routine sleep schedule and ensure they are falling asleep and waking up at the same time every night. Remind, and perhaps help them to keep their room and house clean. A chaotic environment creates a chaotic mind, so keeping their environment clean and organized can help keep their thoughts the same way.

Accept Your Own Limits

Everybody has their limits, including you. Don't allow yourself to believe that the success of your loved one's treatment relies solely on you. It is their job and their responsibility to put the work in to recover, not yours. Don't make it your sole responsibility to rescue them every time they are in crisis. Unless they are your spouse or your child, there are other people that can help them within your family. Constantly taking all of the responsibility of their recovery, on top of your own responsibilities, can cause you to burn out very quickly.

Taking on extra responsibilities can leave you feeling drained and can damage your mental and physical health. If you feel the stress of being a caretaker to your loved one is too much to bear, don't be afraid to seek help yourself. You can't pour from an empty cup, so remember to prioritize your mental and physical health also.

Focus on Your Life too

You have to focus on your own life, and allow yourself to come first. Don't be afraid to set boundaries with your loved one and your family. Feel free to tell them 'no' if you can't make time to do something for them because you have previous obligations or plans made. You are allowed to have your own life, even if your child or spouse has a mental illness, that doesn't mean you have to always make them your center of attention.

Being a caretaker can bring a lot of stress into your life. Making sure that you manage your own stress as you try to help your loved one lower theirs can keep you from becoming overstressed and overwhelmed with your new responsibilities. Taking the extra time to be alone and gather your thoughts for even just a few moments isn't a crime, and you shouldn't feel guilty for it.

Chapter 9: Ways to Prevent Future Mood Episodes

Consciously taking actions that could possibly prevent or lessen the severity of a mood episode can make treatment easier and more successful. Simply looking into getting help and different types of treatment are steps towards getting your life back together. Getting help with an illness that can seriously impact every aspect of your life, whether it's a physical or mental illness, isn't something to be ashamed of but should be celebrated. It shows that you love yourself enough to try to get better and deep down you know you deserve to be happy.

Find Treatment as Soon as Possible

By now I am sure that you have seen how damaging an untreated bipolar disorder can be to your life, job, reputation, and relationships. Unfortunately, simply wishing that your symptoms would go away on their own doesn't work. That's why finding treatment as soon as possible is so important to all aspects of your life. Trying to fix all of your symptoms with self-control and willpower isn't going to do any good when some days you don't even have the willpower to bathe. Treatment can help you put the pieces of your life back together as you begin to get better.

Keeping a Regular Sleeping Schedule

Missing a substantial amount of sleep, even for a night, can trigger a manic or depressive episode. Try to make a manageable sleep schedule that allows you to fall asleep and wake up at the same time every day. Sometimes your sleep schedule may need to be adjusted due to work responsibilities or a planned night out, but make sure you get at least eight hours of sleep a night to feel focused and refreshed when you wake up.

Keeping your room clean and comfortable allows you to get a good night's sleep. Waking up to a clean room can start your day off on a good note and with a good mood. If you wake up to a bedroom that looks like it was hit with an atomic bomb, you are going to feel instantly irritated and want to just go back to sleep so you don't have to deal with it.

Try to avoid screen time at least an hour before you go to sleep; this includes televisions, laptops, and cell phones. The blue light emitted from the screens will keep your brain stimulated and make it harder to relax your thoughts in order to fall asleep. Stressful situations, like watching the news or an argument, can make falling asleep hard as well. You will find that your thoughts are racing as you think about what you should have said during the argument or about the traumatic event that you saw on the nightly news; when your thoughts should be slowing down, allowing you to fall asleep.

Pay Attention to Warning Signs

Pay attention to the warning signs that you have become familiar with before a mood episode begins. Realizing that your symptoms have reappeared and what changes may have triggered them can raise your awareness to other possible manic or major depressive symptoms. When the red flags of an oncoming episode pop up, you can warn your family and friends to keep a watchful eye on you. You can then contact your therapist or doctor and see what their advice is for you.

Avoid Drugs and Alcohol

Avoiding drugs and alcohol is a good recommendation for everybody, however, people with bipolar can experience worse symptoms if they partake in the abuse of these substances. You may not share the same experiences as other people when they drink alcohol or abuse drugs. You may become more reclusive or full of rage. Your symptoms will continue to get worse, and the duration of your episodes will last longer and occur more frequently. Drugs and alcohol can interact with your medication terribly and cause you to get very sick, and in some instances, death is a side effect of the interaction. Mixing drugs or alcohol with your medication could also make them ineffective.

Take Your Medication as Directed

Taking your medicine as your doctor directed means that you don't take more than you are supposed to and you don't stop taking it without supervision. Taking more than prescribed can cause an overdose or a severe manic episode, and possibly a psychotic break from reality. A severe episode or psychotic break can place you on a psychiatric hold on suicide watch for days at a time, a fear that most people with mental illness already have. Taking more medication without your doctor's medical advice isn't going to make you feel better.

Deciding to stop taking your medicine abruptly has its own set of issues. Once you start to feel better and your symptoms are manageable, you are going to be tempted to stop taking them. You will start to forget why you were taking them in the first place when you feel so much happier and healthier now. Your progress is largely because of your medication, and you still need to take it so you can keep feeling better and progressing in your recovery. If you stop, your symptoms will undoubtedly come back, and they will possibly come back stronger than before. Certain medications will have you going through withdrawal, as if you were coming off of hard drugs. If you feel like your medication isn't working, contact your doctor directly instead of taking treatment into your own hands. They can slowly wean you off of the medication as they replace it with a new one.

Some people feel the need to stop taking their medication for just one night so that they can have that manic energy as they scramble to finish a project or study for their exams. Other people just miss the joys of having that much energy and how much they were able to accomplish in a small amount of time. Deciding to not take your medicine for even just one day can throw off your entire treatment and be the beginning of a severe episode. You will find the familiar feelings of mania to be euphoric, and maybe start to believe that you don't need your medication anymore as you slowly relapse into your previous ways. Keeping a consistent daily medication routine will help prevent a possible mood episode and keep you from returning back to the destructive behaviors of old.

You will have to constantly battle your mental illness when it tells you that you are fine and you don't need the medicine, but don't believe it. That's what mental illnesses do, that is their job. They make you question yourself and those around you, and the motives surrounding your treatment. They damage your ability to think clearly and rationally, and they distort your beliefs to reflect your biggest fears.

Conclusion

I hope you found this guide to bipolar disorder to be a worthy companion in your journey to recovery. Knowing the difference between each type of bipolar and what all they entail regarding symptoms can give you a fresh perspective on what you or your loved one is dealing with on a daily basis.

Learning about how bipolar disorder is treated and the alternative ways to treat your symptoms at home can give you the tools you need to move forward and improve your mental and emotional wellbeing.

Remembering to be emotionally and physically supportive of your loved one as they work hard to get better can open new doors to the way you communicate and bond with them.

The tips and techniques that you have been provided with in order to prevent future manic and depressive episodes may not always work, but they will allow you to be much more aware of your worsening symptoms and better prepared to get the help you need, as soon as you need it.

References

Anxiety and Depression Association of America. (2021).
    Bipolar Disorder. Adaa.org.
    https://adaa.org/understanding-anxiety/co-occurring-
    disorders/bipolar-disorder#CoOccurring

Calabro, S. (2016, January 15). *9 Natural Therapies for Bipolar*
    Depression. EverydayHealth.com.
    https://www.everydayhealth.com/bipolar-
    disorder/alternative-treatments-for-bipolar-
    disorder.aspx

Center for Discovery. (2019). *Understanding What Actually*
    Happens in EMDR Therapy. Center for Discovery.
    https://centerfordiscovery.com/understanding-actually-
    happens-emdr-therapy/

Chakrabarty, T. (2020, February 26). *Does bipolar disorder*
    damage your brain? CREST.BD.
    https://www.crestbd.ca/2020/02/26/bipolar-brain-
    damage/

Currin-Sheehan, K. (2021, April 29). *Popular Vitamins to*
    Supplement Bipolar Disorder Treatment. Psych Central.
    https://psychcentral.com/bipolar/vitamins-for-bipolar-
    disorder#natural-remedies-to-avoid

DeNoon, D. J. (2005a, March 25). *Antipsychotic Medication*
    for Bipolar Disorder. WebMD; WebMD.

https://www.webmd.com/bipolar-disorder/guide/antipsychotic-medication

DeNoon, D. J. (2005b, March 25). *Bipolar Disorder and Electroconvulsive Therapy (ECT)*. WebMD; WebMD. https://www.webmd.com/bipolar-disorder/guide/electroconvulsive-therapy-ect

DeNoon, D. J. (2005c, March 25). *Medications for Bipolar Disorder*. WebMD; WebMD. https://www.webmd.com/bipolar-disorder/guide/medications-bipolar-disorder

How to Meditate. (2019). Headspace. https://www.headspace.com/meditation/how-to-meditate

Jaret, P. (2008, February 8). *Bipolar Disorder & The Benefits Of Meditation*. BpHope.com. https://www.bphope.com/body-brio-relaxed-in-the-moment/

Mayo Clinic. (2018a). *Cyclothymia (cyclothymic disorder) - Symptoms and causes*. Mayo Clinic; https://www.mayoclinic.org/diseases-conditions/cyclothymia/symptoms-causes/syc-20371275

Mayo Clinic. (2018b, January 31). *Bipolar disorder - Symptoms and causes*. Mayo Clinic; https://www.mayoclinic.org/diseases-conditions/bipolar-disorder/symptoms-causes/syc-20355955

Meissner, M. (2021, July 7). *Meditation for Bipolar Disorder: How to Balance a Healthy Lifestyle*. Psych Central. https://psychcentral.com/bipolar/meditation-and-bipolar-disorder-symptoms#about-meditation

National Alliance on Mental Illness. (2020). *Bipolar disorder | NAMI: National Alliance on Mental Illness*. Nami.org. https://www.nami.org/About-Mental-Illness/Mental-Health-Conditions/Bipolar-Disorder/Treatment

Purse, M. (2020, September 25). *Why Did Manic Depression Become Bipolar Disorder?* Verywell Mind. https://www.verywellmind.com/why-did-manic-depression-become-bipolar-disorder-379822

Roland, J. (2016, April 7). *Bipolar 1 vs. Bipolar 2: Know the Difference*. Healthline. https://www.healthline.com/health/bipolar-disorder/bipolar-1-vs-bipolar-2#causes

Smith, M., & Segal, J. (2020, September). *Helping Someone With Bipolar Disorder*. HelpGuide. https://www.helpguide.org/articles/bipolar-disorder/helping-someone-with-bipolar-disorder.htm